Contents

KU-023-950

I am a postman   4

The mail centre   6

The sorting office   8

Coffee break   10

Delivering mail   12

Happy birthday!   14

More deliveries   16

Special Deliveries   18

Postboxes   20

Back to the mail centre   22

Glossary   23

Index   24

I am a postman

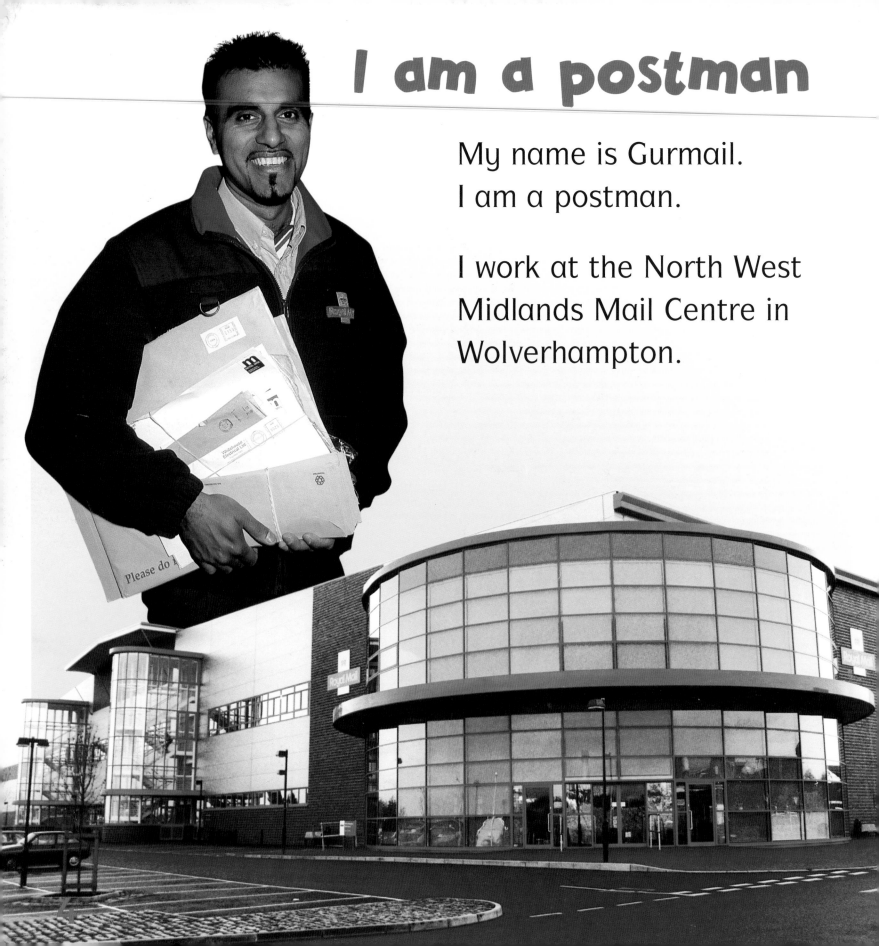

My name is Gurmail.
I am a postman.

I work at the North West Midlands Mail Centre in Wolverhampton.

POSTMAN

Rebecca Hunter

**Photography by
Chris Fairclough**

CHERRYTREE BOOKS

A Cherrytree book

First published in paperback in 2011 by
Evans Brothers Ltd
2A Portman Mansions
Chiltern Street
London W1U 6NR

British Library Cataloguing in Publication Data
Hunter, Rebecca
   Postman. - (People who help us)
   1. Letters carriers - Juvenile literature
   I. Title
   383. 1

ISBN 9781842346297

Planned and produced by Discovery Books Ltd
Editor: Rebecca Hunter
Designer: Ian Winton
© Evans Brothers Ltd 2005

Acknowledgements
Commissioned photography by Chris Fairclough.

The author, packager and publisher would like to thank Gurmail Singh, Jane Thomas, Lin Green
and the North West Midlands Mail Centre.

Printed in India by Nutech Print Services.

Words appearing in bold **like this**, are explained in the glossary.

A **mail centre** is a very busy place.
About one thousand postal workers
work here. Over two million letters and
parcels pass through here every day.

The mail centre

5am I arrive at the mail centre very early in the morning. It is often still dark.

This is the inside of the mail centre. It is very busy here, all day and all night.

Lorries and vans are arriving all the time with mail to be sorted. This is Claire. She is unloading a delivery of mail.

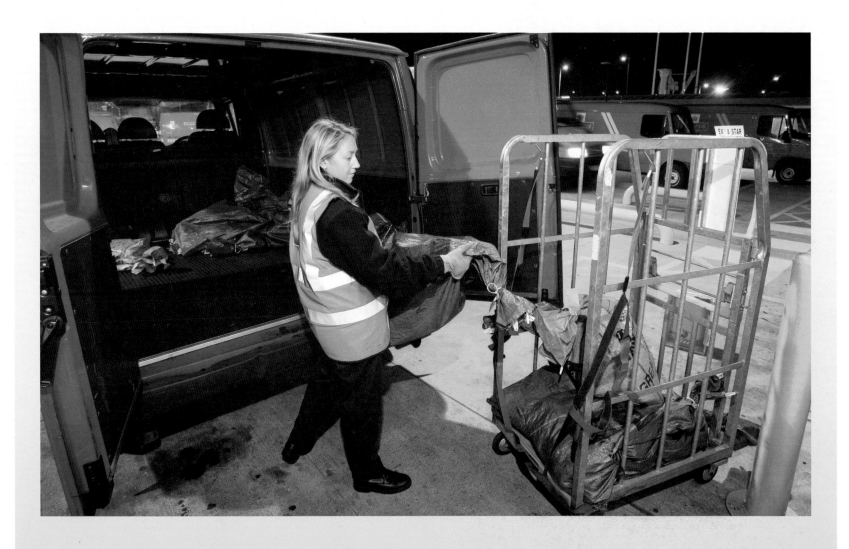

The mail will be sorted in the mail centre by **postcode** and sent around the country and abroad.

The sorting office

This is the **sorting office** for the Wolverhampton area. I have to sort the letters for my area into a rack called a frame. There is a slot for every single address.

It helps me if the letters are addressed properly. A well-addressed letter always shows the postcode.

Miss Sophie Smith
25 Beech Avenue
WOLVERHAMPTON
WV6 2BH

This is a first class stamp.

This is the postcode.

Putting a first class stamp on a letter means it will arrive sooner.

Sometimes **Royal Mail** brings out **special editions** of stamps.

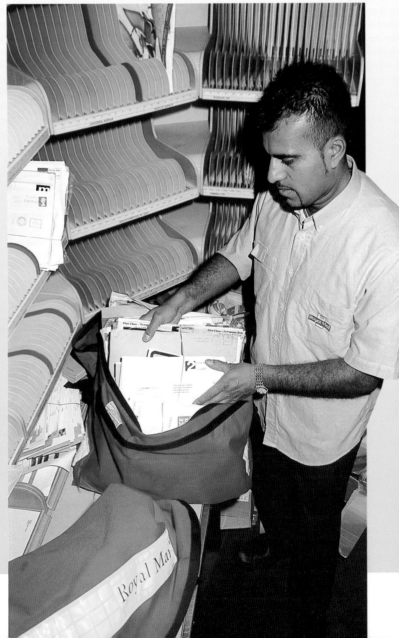

Here is a set with woodland animals. Many people enjoy collecting these special sets.

I collect the letters together in groups for each street and put them in my bag.

Coffee break

6.30 Because I have finished sorting my letters early, I have time for a break. I get a cup of coffee from the machine and have a chat with some other postal workers.

I put on my **reflective** jacket, so that I can be seen in the dark. I put my mail bags on a trolley and push it down to my van.

I put the bags of mail into the back of my van.

Now I am ready to do my deliveries.

Delivering mail

I deliver letters to 400 homes and businesses. I park my van and take the letters I need for the first road.

I walk up and down the road, delivering the mail to each house in turn.

There are many different types of house on my round.

Some are very large, others are quite small. Some houses have lovely gardens.

All the houses have one important thing a postman needs – a letter box!

Happy birthday!

I have a lot of letters and parcels for this house. I think it must be someone's birthday.

The whole family comes to the door. They tell me it is Kialli's birthday. She is seven years old today.

Kialli is happy that so many people have remembered her birthday.

I wonder what is in the parcel?

More deliveries

My next delivery is to a school. This school often has a lot of post.

I have a chat with the school **receptionist**. She is always happy to see me.

This household owns a dog.
The dog is nice and friendly.
Unfortunately not all dogs
are friendly. I have been
barked at, growled at and
bitten several times!

Here is a block of flats.
I have to go to each
flat on three floors.
Being a postman
keeps me quite fit.

Special Deliveries

Some letters are **Special Delivery**. This means someone has to **sign** for them, to show they have been delivered, and on time.

I have a Special Delivery for this business. Luckily someone is here and can sign for it.

I have another Special
Delivery for this address.
I ring the doorbell
but nobody
answers.

I leave a card to say they
have a Special Delivery.
They will have to go to
pick up the delivery from
the sorting office.

Postboxes

I have finished my deliveries but I still have one more thing to do. I have to empty some postboxes.

This woman is just in time. She posts her letter before I empty the box.

Each postbox has a time label on it. This tells you when the last pick-up will be from the box each day. The time on this box says 6.15pm.

I have some keys to open the postboxes. I take out the letters and put them in my sack.

I will take them back to the mail centre.

Back to the mail centre

12.30 I go back to the mail centre. I hand in the letters I have just collected, ready to be sorted.

I have one last thing to do. I have to return the Special Delivery that I could not deliver. I have to sign my name to show I have returned it.

Now it is time to go home. It is only lunchtime, but I have been up for eight hours. It is hard work being a postman but I really enjoy it.

Glossary

mail centre a large regional office where machines sort mail to be sent to sorting offices

postcode a series of letters and numbers that help Royal Mail sort mail

receptionist a person who works in an office, answers the phone and greets visitors

reflective something that shines back light

Royal Mail a company which collects, sorts and delivers letters and parcels

sign to write your name on something

sorting office a small local office where postmen and women sort mail before it is delivered

Special Delivery a service used to send important and valuable items through the post

special edition a set of stamps that people can collect

Index

addresses 8

coffee break 10
collections 20, 21

dogs 17

letters 5, 8, 9, 12, 13, 20, 21, 22

mail bags 9, 11
mail centre 4, 5, 6, 7, 21, 22

parcels 4, 5, 14, 15
postal workers 5, 6, 7, 10
post round 12, 13, 14, 15, 16, 17, 18, 19
post van 7, 11, 12
postboxes 20, 21
postcodes 7, 8

reflective jacket 11
Royal Mail 9

school delivery 16
sorting office 8, 9
Special Deliveries 18, 19, 22
special editions 9
stamps 8, 9